TAE KWON DOG

THE POWER WITHIN

Illustration and design by Susan Szecsi
www.brainmonsters.com

ISBN: 9780578771588 (paperback)
ISBN: 9780578771595 (ebook)

Published in 2021 by Diane DiRoberto
Printed in the United States of America

TAE KWON DOG
THE POWER WITHIN

STORY BY DIANE DIROBERTO

ILLUSTRATIONS BY SUSAN SZECSI

Acknowledgments

I am filled with gratitude to these awesome folks who helped me realize my dream of writing *Tae Kwon Dog: The Power Within*...

Old friends **Daryl and Fred Black** for their unwavering patience while training me in *Tae Kwon Do*. As an adult student, I was humbled by my lack of experience yet grew more confident after each lesson with Daryl. Fred may be surprised to know his encouraging words inspired the creation of the character *Tae Kwon Dog*.

My good buddy and sounding board for all things creative **Judith A. Adamson** for editing the early pages of *Tae Kwon Dog: The Power Within*.

Editor **Fiona Simpson** for her keen eye and thoughtful suggestions that helped make this book the very best version of itself.

Designer and illustrator **Susan Szecsi** for drawing *Tae Kwon Dog* and the rest of the crew as I envisioned them and bringing them to life for us to enjoy.

My loving family and friends who cheered me on while writing this book—especially my aunts **Sylvia DiRoberto** and **Julia M. Hill** whose excitement for its completion rivaled my own.

Contents

Dedicated to my dog Otto
who lives in my heart forever.

This book is also dedicated to everyone
who believes dogs are smarter than humans
because they are loyal, forgiving
and love us just as we are.

CHAPTER ONE

Welcome to the Dojang

In a small changing room in a martial arts studio called 'the dojang', the Tae Kwon Do instructor prepares for his next class. He studies his reflection in the mirror as he puts on his oversized pajama-like uniform. It looks two sizes too big for his compact muscular body which stands about three feet tall. Next he carefully winds a long black belt around his waist, making sure both ends hang down evenly. He hasn't always liked his reflection, but today he no longer sees himself as the runt-of-the-litter pup who once feared for his life in the city pound. Now the dog in the mirror is strong, healthy, and powerful. Maybe even handsome, but it makes him shy to think so. When he's done, he bows to himself in the mirror and smiles. He is a 9th Dan black belt – the highest level of achievement in the martial art of Tae Kwon Do. He is the master of his own dojang. And he is a dog. Life is sweet.

Tae Kwon Dog looks at the world through large chocolate eyes with an intelligence similar to that of a well-schooled human being. Given his quiet nature, some may think he doesn't have much to say, but they would be wrong. When he speaks, he does so softly and intently, and he never barks—unless it's absolutely necessary.

His short dark coat is always clean, shiny, and smooth. And with his deep caramel-colored markings, he looks confident and regal—not at all like the bone-thin, nearly bald little dog he used to be. However, because of his past, his sharp black nose is super-sensitive not only to smells like food or fire, but also to emotions like embarrassment, sadness, and loneliness. He is especially quick to smell danger.

Soft morning light streams into the spacious white room from a wall of windows that looks out on the dojang's peaceful, park-like courtyard. Wind chimes caught in a gentle breeze and birds chirping hello to one another are the only sounds that can be heard.

Mirrors line another wall so the students can study their reflections as they begin their instruction. The gleaming hardwood floors are kept spotlessly clean and the room is empty except for a tall stack of green exercise mats and wood training swords called 'bokkens' racked up on the wall.

Tae Kwon Dog enters and bows before two flags hanging at the front of the room. The red, white, and blue American flag in all its glory hangs proudly next to the South Korean flag in bold colors of red, blue, black, and white. The martial art form known today as Tae Kwon Do began many centuries ago

in Korea which is in East Asia.

The dojang's silence is broken by a group of young students pouring through the door. Already dressed in their crisp white uniforms, they quickly remove their shoes and place them neatly in a row at the entrance. Barefoot, they throw a few playful kicks at each other before grabbing a mat and sitting cross-legged on the floor facing the flags. Their belts are tied exactly like the Master's, but are blue instead of black, showing that they are serious, intermediate students of Tae Kwon Do. Over their hearts is a school patch that Tae Kwon Dog has given them as a reward for their hard work.

The room grows quiet again as the Master writes today's exercise on the blackboard. When he turns to face the group, they all jump up from their mats and stand at attention. Each student places their hand over their heart and bows to honor the flags. Then, with arms at their sides, the students close their eyes for a brief time of quiet called 'meditation' which helps them focus on what they are about to learn.

Not long ago, the idea of a dog teaching Tae Kwon Do to a roomful of children would have been unthinkable. Now in the 21st century, after decades of bad human behavior, animals have been forced to speak out. All over the world, they have begun using their native languages to express their keen understanding of life and the universe. Dogs, the most intuitive and intelligent of any species on earth, have communicated their ability to understand humans and have become our most trusted and valuable advisors, teachers, and world leaders.

Now the whole room is moving as the students warm up their muscles before beginning today's lesson. Some are on their mats doing push-ups and stomach crunches, while others swing their legs high in the air, practicing their kicks. All are excited to work on a Tae Kwon Do Technique called "Horse Stance Punch".

At the front of the room, Tae Kwon Dog demonstrates the stance. The students watch him attentively and mimic his actions. The master then walks through the class watching each student perform the movement.

Suddenly, a shadow figure outside the window catches his eye. As the class keeps practicing, the Master quietly leaves the room to investigate. He finds himself face to face with a huge gray dog who is half hidden behind a tree.

"May I help you?" asks Tae Kwon Dog, moving closer to the dog who's easily three times his size. The mysterious dog stays quiet, eyes lowered, almost as if trying to be invisible.

"What is your name?" the Master persists.

The towering canine jerks his leg up and

begins scratching himself uncontrollably.

"I, um, am Max. I'm sorry I interrupted your class."

"Not to worry, Max. Would you like to come in and join us?" the Master asks the seemingly shy dog.

"No, uh, I have to go home." says Max softly, slowing backing away. "My owner will be looking for me."

The Master regards Max kindly as he slowly moves out from under the tree and starts off in the opposite direction.

"You're welcome to come back any time Max." Tae Kwon Dog calls after him as Max slowly wanders down the road, big floppy ears swaying with each step, his long scraggily tail brown with dirt dragging on the ground behind him.

At an auto repair shop just a few blocks from the dojang, Max lies panting by a pile of old tires roasting in the hot sun. When he sees his human Dan lock the shop door and start off down the street, Max pulls himself up and quickly falls in step with him.

"Oh, there you are buddy. I thought you left town," jokes the lanky young man as he reaches into the pocket of his greasy, gasoline-smelling shirt and tosses Max a treat.

"How about splitting a tuna sandwich with me?"

Max is hungry and barks his approval. He knows that after work Dan will be so tired that he'll probably fall asleep at this desk and forget to eat dinner. And like usual, he probably won't take Max for a walk or remember to feed him until morning. Max doesn't get mad. Dan works hard and he just forgets some times, thinks Max.

Later that night, after dumpster-diving for leftovers at Pizza Perfecto across the street, Max burps and savors the taste of pepperoni on his tongue. It's still hot outside on this muggy summer night and he's not ready to go home just yet. Wandering the streets, he stops and sniffs at his favorite spots and eventually finds himself back at the dojang.

Other than a small golden light over the front door, the building is dark and quiet. Max finds a comfy patch of cool grass in the courtyard and lies down. Before long he falls into a deep sleep. His eyes twitch and his legs race beneath him. In his dream, he's no longer the large lumbering dog with thin hair, itchy skin, and a scraggily tail. He's slender and strong and moves with the grace of a tiger.

CHAPTER TWO

The Master's Way

Early on a Saturday morning, the dojang is buzzing with activity as the Master's advanced class tests for their first black belt promotion. Seated on benches, uniformed students wait patiently for their turn to present their solo program while a standing-room-only crowd of proud parents looks on.

At the front of the room, Tae Kwon Dog sits at a long table with a well-worn leather record book open in front of him. He fingers its pages gently, careful not to rip them. These pages hold the names of every student who has been promoted at the dojang from his first days as Master. The students sit patiently, eyeing the black belts stacked on the side of the table. Each of them hopes to earn a belt on this very special day.

When Tae Kwon Dog calls out a student's name, the young martial artist runs to the center of the room and crouches down with head bowed and touching the floor in a show of respect. Tae Kwon Do in Korean means 'the way of kicking and punching'. Part self-defense and part sport, the martial art can also be a form of artistic expression, and the Master encourages his students to put their personalities into their performances.

Today, the students have chosen music to accompany their solo programs. A teenage girl, blonde hair tied in a knot atop her head, moves with deliberate grace to a thundering Beethoven concerto, another student breakdances to his favorite hip-hop tune in between the required kicks and blocks. Rounds of applause follow each performance as the students express their support for one another. Now, as the last student begins, the room is silent.

Standing just four feet tall, Caleb is the smallest competitor. His dark eyes peek through a curtain of shiny black hair. A small silver dragon on rawhide sits at his throat. He bows and makes direct eye contact with the Master. As the theme from Mission Impossible begins, Tae Kwon Dog suppresses a smile. Caleb reminds the Master of himself early in his training. His slight frame gives him the advantage of speed and agility, but he has had to work harder than most to develop his strength and at times

it has been painful. Now his confidence shows as he moves through his program, punctuating every punch, block, and kick with a distinctive grunt. He finishes with a backflip, followed by a cartwheel and lands firmly on both feet. Hoots, whistles, and cheers of approval follow Caleb as he returns to the bench and takes his place next to the others.

At the end of every promotion, the Master demonstrates his exceptional skill as a 9th Dan black belt. His flowing circular movements are seamless; his jumps strong and fast, and his kicks powerful and precise. The room is quiet as Tae Kwon Dog spins swiftly in the air, landing a solid back kick that splits a 6-inch board held high by two visiting black belts. Then he quickly turns his attention to a stack of bricks set up nearby.

With a loud 'Hup!', he plows through them with his right front paw and the broken bricks drop to the floor. The stillness in the room explodes into applause as the Master bows to the crowd. His jaw-dropping performance has everyone on their feet.

CHAPTER THREE

Be True to Yourself

Across town, Max is stretched out enjoying the cool protection of an old shade tree on the front lawn of Myer's Corner Store. On hot summer days, this is his favorite spot to watch the world go by. It's far enough away from the loud rumbling swamp cooler at the auto repair and the sickening smell of the old tires out back. Since his neighborhood is in the industrial part of town, surrounded by warehouses and factories, there's little relief from the heat and the sizzling sidewalks that burn his paws. Dan likes to say, "You could fry an egg on that sidewalk". Max wishes he could fry Dan an egg sandwich and split it with him, but he doesn't know how to cook.

Max used to meet his good friend Monty under this same tree every Saturday morning. Monty, a handsome Golden Retriever with an enviable fluffy tail, was often covered in dust from his human's studio. She was an artist who made gigantic sculptures of nothing Max could recognize. One day a sad Monty told Max that his human had been invited to work in Japan. At first, he said he was happy for her and excited to go, until she tearfully confessed that she wouldn't be able to take him with her. It's been weeks now, but Max still stares in Monty's direction hoping to see him, tail held high, walking down the road.

Out of the corner of one eye Max sees the Ratwailer brothers, two huge and beefy Rottweiler purebreds, loping toward him. He immediately senses trouble but pretends not to notice them.

"Hey Max?" croaks Rufus, the larger of the two. Both are wearing thick dark leather collars with sharp silver studs that stick out in a menacing way. Max slowly looks up in their direction and nods. Soon they're standing on either side of him.

"What's up?" asks Max.

"Not much," says Squeaky. He is short and stocky, and his name comes from his wheezy, high-pitched voice which sounds a bit like a door that needs oiling.

"We're just going to the store to pick up a few things, wanna join us?" The brothers glance at each other and let out loud, sinister snorts in unison.

"I think I'll pass guys, I'm pretty comfortable right here," says Max.

"Suit yourself," says Rufus, shrugging his shoulders.

Max watches as they disappear into the store. After a few minutes, a curious Max pulls himself up and goes over to peek in the store's window. As he suspected, he sees the brothers helping themselves to an entire display of beef jerky. Knowing there's going to be trouble, Max heads back to the auto shop. Soon the brothers appear chomping on the jerky.

"Hey Max, check this out," wails Squeaky. He has a new music player hanging around his neck with little silver headphones stuck in his hairy ears.

"Old man Myers can't hear a thing, let alone see anything," rumbles Rufus.

"You stole that!" Max shouts then starts scratching himself feverishly.

"Yeah, so what? Stores expect some stealing, that's why they charge such high prices," squeaks Squeaky.

"Grrrright," wisecracks Rufus, "Squeaky, let's go hang out with Max."

Max shakes his head and starts fast walking down the road with the Ratwailer brothers following closely behind.

"Wow, look at that sweet ride!" cries Squeaky, pointing to a bright, shiny red convertible in the auto repair shop.

"That's Mayor Richards's vintage sports car. Dan's restoring it for him," says Max.

"Looks like it's ready for a test drive!" exclaims a mischievous Rufus.

"No, Dan's still working on it, and besides, he's the only one who can drive it."

Max is getting uneasy and wishes the brothers would just leave, but he doesn't want to make them mad by asking.

"Oh, come on Max, just a little spin around the block, we'll be careful," Rufus says, laughing gruffly.

"Yeah, yeah let's go for a ride!" Squeaky adds excitedly.

Rufus eyes the lever for the hydraulic lift. He grabs it and yanks it down hard, letting the car fall to the ground with a rough bounce.

"Hey! Hey! Hey!" shouts Rufus, "she's ready to go. Where's the keys, man?"

"I don't know," lies Max, trying not to

look at the hook where the keys are hanging. If only Dan was here. He left for the city early in the morning and probably won't be back before dark.

Rufus spies a gold key hanging alone on a hook above the workbench. He smiles and grabs it, waving it in the air.

"Could this be it? Let's go for a grrrride!"

"No, Rufus," pleads Max, "do you even know how to drive?"

Rufus jumps in the right-hand drive roadster and Squeaky piles in the passenger side after him.

"Sure Max, I'm a regular at the Indy 500!" Rufus barks as he tries to start the car.

In a minute he has the car in reverse and peels out of the shop. Desperate to stop them, Max leaps into the car, squeezing into the small back seat, meant for luggage not people.

With gears grinding, the shiny red convertible jerks out of the parking lot and begins rocketing through town. Flying down the street, the crazed dogs pass the astonished faces of pedestrians as they run to get out of the way of the speeding convertible.

"Please oh please, we gotta go back!" cries Max.

Ignoring Max's pleas, Rufus puts the pedal to the metal, taking an open road out of town. Max is hoping they'll run out of gas soon, but it's not soon enough.

"This is what I'm talking about!" screams Rufus.

"Yeah, man!" Squeaky squeals with delight.

Coming to a fork in the road, a confused Rufus turns too sharply, sending

the car spinning wildly out of control. Rolling off the road's rocky shoulder, the car rams through a guardrail before heading into a field where several black-and-white spotted Holstein cows are quietly grazing. On seeing the car careening toward them, the nervous cows run for cover. There's no way to avoid a white picket fence in their path, so the three dogs jump out just in time before the convertible crashes into it.

In the distance, a man, dressed in overalls and carrying a shotgun in his hands, comes running in their direction. Seeing this, Rufus and Squeaky take off on all fours, scrambling madly for the road. The man fires two shots in their direction as he advances toward Max, who's shaking his head to clear it, the ground still spinning beneath him.

Max pulls himself up and stands dutifully beside the steaming wreck which had once been the Mayor's pride and joy.

As the man approaches, the shotgun tucked firmly under his arm, Max resists the urge to scratch wildly. He's scared and feels just like he did years ago at the city pound, before Dan took him home. Now he's afraid Dan will be so mad, that he'll take him back to the pound.

"How did I let this happen?" Max worries aloud to himself. For the life of him, he doesn't know. But what he does know is that this time he's reached the end of the road.

Late that night, a whistling Dan unlocks the door to his garage and turns on the light. The first thing he sees is Max lying on the floor, almost lifeless, with his right, front leg in a bright blue cast. In the next moment he notices the Mayor's vintage car missing from the lift.

"What the... Max? What's going on here? What happened to you? Where's the Mayor's car?"

Max struggles to get up and ambles over with his tail between his legs.

"I'm so..." is all Max can muster before throwing up on Dan's good dress shoes.

"Max! For mercy's sakes, what's wrong with you?" cries a confused and upset Dan.

Scared and shaking, Max can barely look at Dan, but he knows he has to tell him what happened. After all, he was responsible and regardless of what happens next, he must tell him the truth, even it means being sent back to the pound... and he knows what that meant for an older dog with a broken leg—and not a particularly cute dog at that!

Dan lowers himself to the floor as a wet-eyed Max begins to tell him everything that happened. From running into the crazy Ratwailer Brothers and how they followed him back to the garage. Dan listens carefully, but there's no expression on his face. Why is his face like that Max wonders? He usually smiles when he looks at me. He must really be mad, Max thinks to himself. Then he tells him about Rufus and Squeaky stealing the Mayor's car and crashing into the farmer's fence.

Dan's eyes grow large when he hears about the car, but he lets Max finish his story. Max tells him about the farmer coming out with the gun, and how the brothers left him there to face the angry man alone.

Dan takes off his cap and scratches his head.

"How'd you get the cast on your leg?"

"The farmer saw I was limping and dropped me off at the Vet. Dr. Drake put the cast on and said he'd take it out with you in trade—whatever that means."

Dan's silence makes Max more nervous. He resists the urge to scratch, thinking any movement might make Dan even madder. Instead, he sits quietly with his ears curled back in a humbled position.

Finally, Dan gets up and grabs the phone. He calls the owner of the farm where the Ratwailers crashed the car. He knows the farmer can be ornery, but he's a fair and decent man.

"Yes, that's the Mayor's car. I plan to tow it first thing in the morning, sir. I'll pay for any damages... yes, to your fence and... oh, I'm sorry your cows were frightened... well, please let me know what I can do to make things right."

Dan hangs up the phone and looks crossly at Max who is standing on his three good legs. Then he sighs heavily.

"Once I size up the damage, I'll call the Mayor. You better bed down, Max," says Dan pointing to a beat-up old dog bed shoved in the corner by the car lift. It belonged to Dan's last dog, and Max only lies on it when he watches Dan work. Now, he limps over and collapses on the thread-bare cushion. Since Dan brought him home, he's never slept overnight in the garage.

Dan turns out the light and closes the door behind him. Max is heartsick. He knows

he's let Dan down—big time. After a long minute, the door opens and Max hears Dan's familiar whistle, calling him into the house.

☆ CHAPTER FOUR ☆

Nobody's Perfect

On weekends Tae Kwon Dog swaps his martial arts uniform for jeans and sneakers and leaves the dojang for the day to enjoy his favorite hobby—taking pictures. It's a short train ride into New York City where there is so much to see and photograph with his new Digi-dog camera. As soon as he gets to Manhattan, he hightails it over to Central Bark—the coolest dog park right in the middle of

Central Park. On the way, he stops to feed the ducks and swans on the lake and snaps a few shots of rowers gliding along the water, with the city's skyline behind them.

The park is a magical place where everyone is welcome and the view from every bench is awesome. At the park zoo, he often gets a few friends to pose for a portrait or two. Other times, the talented jugglers and street musicians are his inspiration. For lunch he'll munch on a mustard and sauerkraut hotdog while watching a baseball game.

Today as he runs down the grassy field into Central Bark, he senses trouble ahead. Two big, beefy black dogs in studded collars are sniffing around a picnic table. A tall thin man and a large grey dog with a cast on his front leg are obviously not happy with the attention their lunch is getting from the intruders. As he gets closer, Tae Kwon Dog recognizes the large grey dog as Max, the same dog that had been outside his dojang just a few weeks before.

The menacing dogs are out to steal their lunch, and even though Max himself is a big guy, the poor injured dog is no match for them.

"Get out of here!" The man yells as the dogs pull their food to the ground. "Max are these the same dogs that stole and crashed the Mayor's car? Get away, you thugs!"

With only three legs to balance on, Max is unsteady and the muscular black dogs are getting the best of him.

"Leave us alone!" Max cries. "Haven't you Ratwailers made my life miserable enough?"

Max swings his big blue cast at them as the bigger one of the bullying dogs tries to grab it.

"Hey Max, let's see how rrrruff and

ttttuff you are with one paw tied behind your back!" teases Rufus.

Tae Kwon Dog quickly stashes his camera behind a tree and dashes down the hill. When they see the compact canine running toward them, the Ratwailers stop bothering Max and howl with laughter.

"What's this?" barks Rufus.

"Looks like an appeteaser to me!" snorts Squeaky.

The Master musters all his mental energy as he spins swiftly in the air and delivers a crushing blow to a nearby boulder with his bare paw. The trouble-making dogs gape open-mouthed as the boulder shatters into pebbles at their feet. They look at each other in disbelief before bolting up the hill and heading out of the park.

"How'd you do that?" Max cries in amazement.

"Never underestimate the power within," replies Tae Kwon Dog calmly.

"You're quite a powerhouse!" says Dan. "You saved my dog—and our food! How can we thank you?"

"Well, wait one minute and I'll show you." says Tae Kwon Dog as he disappears up the hill and returns just as fast with his camera.

"Just let me take your picture! And, maybe there's one more thing."

"Name it!" says Dan.

"Send Max over to my studio. I'd like to teach him how to defend himself."

Max looks up at Dan, then scratches himself nervously.

"It's a deal," Dan says, shaking Tae

Kwon Dog's paw.

"Please, join us for lunch! I think there's still plenty of food," says Dan looking at the ground littered with sandwiches and half-open containers.

"Oh, that's very kind, but I'll be on my way home now. I've had quite enough excitement for one day!" says a smiling Tae Kwon Dog.

"Besides, I don't think I've seen the last of those Ratwailers and I might just have to teach them another lesson," laughs the Master, his eyes shining with anticipation. "Max, I'll see you next week."

"But what about my leg?" asks a reluctant Max.

"No worries, Max. Nobody's perfect. We all come to the dojang with our worries and struggles, but we leave them with our shoes at the front door," says Tae Kwon Dog happily before snapping a photo of his two new friends.

Max isn't sure what Tae Kwon Dog means, he doesn't even wear shoes, but he sees Dan smile and if whatever Tae Kwon

Dog said made Dan happy, he'll do it. Dan had been angry about the Mayor's car, but he forgave him—and he didn't send him back to the scary pound.

He told Max they were family and were together for better or worse. Max guessed he was the worse.

On his way out, Tae Kwon Dog spots the Ratwailer brothers, surrounded by a bunch of scruffy, streetwise city dogs, hanging out at the only exit in Central Bark. When they see him, the Ratwailers sneer and growl menacingly sending the other dogs cowering and running off in all directions.

Tae Kwon Dog just smiles. He is not afraid. He has a secret weapon, and he is confident he has the skills to protect himself against those who would harm him. Though, as a compassionate Master with deep concerns for others, he listens to his heart first, especially in dangerous situations. He knows the Ratwailers act like bullies because they know they are feared. They are big, muscular, and kind of mean-looking so other dogs usually run from them. Because of the way they look, the brothers don't think they are likable or even lovable.

As he approaches the wildly barking brothers, Tae Kwon Dog stays calm and stands directly in front of them.

"Never underestimate the power within!" The Master's voice booms shaking the menacing dogs to their bones. His voice sounds like it is all around them. And with that, the Master spins out of sight before their eyes.

"Whoa... where did he go?" cries Squeaky in disbelief.

"I'm right here behind you and ready to shoot!" shouts Tae Kwon Dog.

The stunned Ratwailers quickly turn around as the Master seizes the moment, aims, and shoots.

"Let me show you Ratwailers what you really look like!" Tae Kwon Dog shouts holding up his camera.

"Wow!" exclaims Rufus. "I didn't know we were so handsome!"

"We look awesome!" croons Squeaky. "Can we get a copy of this for our Mom?"

"Yes, but only under one condition" says the Master, smiling from ear to ear.

"What condition?" asks Rufus hesitantly.

"You have to agree to come and take lessons from me at the dojang."

"Will you teach us your secret power?" begs an excited Squeaky.

"Even better, boys. You'll see you each have your own secret power," confides Tae Kwon Dog.

The wide-eyed Ratwailers look at each other and shout, "Grrrreat! We'll be there."

Back at the dojang the Master sits comfortably in his chair admiring the photos he took in New York City. Over the years he's become quite a good photographer and loves the connection he feels with nature and all living things through the lens of his camera. He carefully examines the pictures one by one. A close-up of a butterfly shows all its brilliant colors. Then there's the rollerbladers, jugglers, monkeys, musicians, and rowers—and yes, that pretty dachshund in the pink rhinestone collar. He

loves the photo of Dan and Max and has a feeling they will become good friends. His favorite, though, is the one of the grinning Ratwailer brothers.

Tae Kwon Dog can't wait to see Max's reaction when the brothers show up to train with him this week. He smiles to himself and closes his eyes.

CHAPTER FIVE

The Road Home

It is sunrise when the Master awakens in his favorite wing-back chair. He is surprised that he never went to bed, but instead had slept the whole night sitting upright. He realizes he must have drifted off after looking at so many photographs. As he wipes the sleep from his eyes, he feels they are moist and begins to remember the dream he had—a dream about his life long, long ago.

In the dream, he was just a young pup. His older sister Daisy, a stately Doberman who was adopted along with him at the shelter by his human family, was running back and forth along the banks of the river, barking at an overturned canoe about thirty feet out in the water. He recognized the faded yellow and white stripes on its side and the barely visible red lettering that said 'Old Yeller'—a joke his humans shared with their grandfather who had owned the boat before them. 'Pops', as they referred to him, had trouble hearing and often spoke too loudly, even in quiet places like church or movie theaters.

Neither Tae Kwon Dog nor Daisy were great swimmers, but he jumped into the icy cold water and dog-paddled as fast as he could toward the distressed boat. Even before he reached it, he could see there was no one in it. He circled it once and even tried looking under it, but his humans were nowhere in sight.

He quickly swam back to the riverbank, teeth-chattering and shivering uncontrollably as he climbed out of the water. Unsure where their family was, the two worried dogs barked until nightfall, hoping someone would hear them and come. Finally, a frantic Daisy took off running. She was so much bigger and faster, Tae Kwon Dog couldn't keep up with her, and she disappeared into the darkness.

After a while, he gave up chasing after her and wandered alone, cold and confused, down an old country road. At dawn's light he saw a shiny white pickup truck. It stopped just a few feet past him, and a young muscular man got out. He smelled of fresh coffee and spoke to him quietly, letting him sniff his hand before gently stroking his head.

"You must be freezing, little buddy." the man said, then picked him up— muddy coat and all—wrapped him in a towel from the truck, and put him on the seat next to him.

Tae Kwon Dog kept looking out the window for any sign of his sister, but after a while he grew tired and fell asleep. When he woke up again, it was to a different life.

Even though his new humans had no children of their own, they had three other mixed breed dogs of different colors and sizes, and two black indoor cats who pretty much kept to themselves. They made him feel welcome right away and cared for him like he was a member of their family while searching to find his humans. Only one person answered the ad they had put in the paper for a dog of his description, but the woman was looking for a lost female.

Each day Tae Kwon Dog felt more comfortable in his new home. He was well fed, played hard with his new siblings, and had his own comfy bed next to the fireplace. In time he grew to love them, though he never forgot his first humans and often wondered where they were, and if they still thought of him.

Now years later, as an enlightened Master, he knows many things happen for a reason. His new family owned a martial arts studio in town and since he was such a friendly dog, they brought him to work every day to greet students as they came into their dojang. It was there he learned to practice Tae Kwon Do and eventually became the first canine black belt, a wise Master, and the keeper of a magical and magnificent secret.

CHAPTER SIX

We Are One

After his wild dream, Tae Kwon Dog sits quietly enjoying his morning coffee. Suddenly the brass bell at the front door rings. He takes a last sip, cleans his cup, and puts it back on the shelf before answering the door. Outside Max shifts back and forth on his three good legs. His cast will come off soon, but it's still a nuisance, and he feels awkward holding his leg out in front of himself.

When Tae Kwon Dog opens the door, a wide smile crosses his face.

"Welcome, Max, please come in."

Max nods hesitantly and limps inside.

"We will practice in this room." says Tae Kwon Dog as he leads Max down the hall into the dojang. Max gawks at the hugeness of it. The ceilings are super high and pitched at the center with big windows on either side that show the clouds rolling by. And the wood floors are so clean, they gleam! Floor-to-ceiling mirrors line one wall and two large flags dominate another —the American Flag and another Max has never seen before. It is almost too much for him to take in. The dojang is so different from any place he's ever been. It is very different from Dan's garage... there isn't a smelly tire in sight!

Max thinks he's in a special place, and he feels special being here.

"I have a dobok for you, Max. That is the uniform we wear to practice Tae Kwon Do," says the Master as he watches Max take in his new surroundings.

"It's hanging in there", he says, pointing to his office. "Why don't you go in and put it on. And don't worry about the belt, I'll show you how to tie it when you come out."

Inside Tae Kwon Dog's office, Max notices the awards and letters of recognition hanging on the walls. On the bookshelf there are belts in many colors and color combinations rolled up neatly in a row next to a framed quote: "A black belt is a white

> # A black belt is
> # a white belt
> # that never quit.

belt that never quit."

Max sees three uniforms hanging on a hook; one with his name pinned to it. He puts on the dobok and studies himself in the mirror. He's nervous about trying something new—especially a sport. He's always been rather clumsy at sports, but he likes how the uniform feels and how he looks in it.

"This is cool!" he says out loud.

Max hears the outside bell ring, and Tae Kwon Dog speaking to someone at the door. The other voices sound familiar, but he's confused. He doesn't know anyone here except Tae Kwon Dog.

Just then the Master opens the door, and Max sees the Ratwailer brothers behind him.

"Max, Rufus and Squeaky will be training with you today. They promised me they would be on their best behavior," says the Master, smiling reassuringly.

Max gulps and smiles weakly.

"Here are your uniforms, boys," says Tae Kwon Dog, motioning to the hangers. "Put them on without the belt and meet us in the dojang."

Inside the dojang the three new students stand in front of the mirror as the Master illustrates the proper way to tie their belts.

"Since you are without knowledge of Tae Kwon Do, your belt is white. It signifies purity—or that you are all beginners, fresh and new," explains Tae Kwon Dog. "As with the Pine Tree, the seed must now be planted and nourished to develop strong roots."

The Ratwailer brothers look at each other and giggle. With their barrel chests and big stomachs, their belts keep slipping down. Regardless of how ridiculous they might look in their uniforms, they don't care. They are here to learn one thing and one thing only: The Master's secret.

Before they begin, the Master hands each of them a sheet of paper.

"Keep this and bring it with you every time we meet. We'll read it before we begin each class—just after we meditate."

"Meditate?" squawks Squeaky with a raised eyebrow.

"What's that?" asks Rufus.

"We will stay quiet for one minute with our eyes closed and our heads bowed. That means no talking, laughing, barking, or scratching. We concentrate on our breathing. It will help us focus and prepare us for our practice," says Tae Kwon Dog.

"Now, close your eyes and listen to your breath, in and out. I'll tell you when to stop."

Tae Kwon Dog knows a minute is a long time to these restless dogs, but they manage to stay still.

"Very good, you may open your eyes," says the Master softly.

"Now, let's read the student creed together," he prompts them, holding up the sheet of paper.

All three students can barely be heard above the Master's strong commanding voice.

"I intend to develop myself in a positive manner and avoid anything that would reduce my mental growth or my physical health.

I intend to develop self-discipline in order to bring out the best in myself and others.

I intend to use what I learn in class to help myself and others and never be hurtful or aggressive."

After reading the creed, Max's paw shoots up.

"Does that mean I can't eat pizza?" he asks earnestly.

The brothers howl with laughter, but stop abruptly when Tae Kwon Dog eyes them sternly.

"I mean, I know it's not good for me," Max continues, "but sometimes, there's not much else to eat."

Tae Kwon Dog considers his question seriously.

"You can eat pizza Max, just maybe not so much of it, okay? You are right to think of eating well as taking care of yourself. The body and the mind are equally important. That's something you brothers might think about."

The Ratwailers stop smiling and scowl at their heavyset reflections in the mirror.

After a long practice session, the three students are tired—but a good tired that comes from playing hard and learning something new. The Master hands each of them a paper cup of cool water.

"You all did very well today. We will meet at the same time on Wednesday, the day after tomorrow."

"Will we learn your secret then, Master?" Rufus asks eagerly.

"In good time, Rufus, in good time," says Tae Kwon Dog, nodding and smiling.

While the three students take off their uniforms and hang them in the Master's office, Squeaky eyes a gold figure of a dog striking a Tae Kwon Do stance on the Master's bookcase. He picks it up and quickly pockets it in his hoodie.

"Hey, put that back!" cries Max.

"Shut up, Max, you goody-goody. He'll never notice. Look at all the stuff he has around here," says Squeaky.

Then the thieving dog whispers in Max's ear, "Tell him, and you're dead meat."

"Why don't you put it back, Squeaky?" growls a bored Rufus. He's doesn't care about the theft, but he's afraid that Tae Kwon Dog might not let them come back, and then they'll never learn his secret.

"No way, Rufus! It's mine now," Squeaky says unapologetically, and with that the brothers bolt out of the room and wave a quick goodbye to Tae Kwon Dog on their way out of the dojang.

Max wants to tell the Master about Squeaky taking the statue, but decides not to. He's afraid the Master may think he's lying and took it himself. Tae Kwon Dog sees that Max is heavy with thought as he leaves the dojang, limping out the door and casting his eyes down as he says goodbye. Max just hopes the Master doesn't notice the statue is missing.

That night the Ratwailer brothers are settled into their bunk beds ready for a good night's sleep after their active day. Squeaky is rubbing the small gold statue when suddenly a strangely familiar voice booms out.

"What you do to me, you do to thee. We are one."

"Who said that?" whispers Squeaky.

"I dunno!" Rufus whispers back.

The voice repeats, "What you do to me,

you do to thee. We are one."

"Oh no! It's the Master—he knows!" cries Rufus.

"You're dreamin'! How can it be him? How can he know?" shouts Squeaky.

"He's got special powers—we know that!" explains Rufus. "We gotta take this back tomorrow morning—first thing, Squeaky! Let's keep the lights on!"

Just after sunrise the brothers wait and watch for Tae Kwon Dog to leave the dojang for his morning run. When he goes out, they sneak in and return the statue to its resting place on the shelf in the Master's office. Just as they're about to leave, the Master appears. He doesn't seem surprised to see them in his office.

"Good morning, boys. Did you forget something?"

"Oh no, ah, I mean yes," stumbles Rufus, avoiding eye contact with the Master. "Squeaky left his music player when he was changing."

Squeaky reaches into his hoodie and holds up the device.

"Oh good, glad you found it," says the Master.

"Yeah, thanks," mumbles Squeaky as they both inch toward the door.

"Hey, before you go, I'd like to show you something."

The Master goes over to the small gold statue and holds it in the palm of his hand.

"I was given this after winning a tournament in Korea. That tournament was one of my most cherished memories because it was the very first time I was allowed to participate as a black belt— and as a canine in a human-dominated sport."

With a little squeeze, the statue speaks. "What you do to me, you do to thee. We are one."

The boys look at each other dumbfounded. They feel foolish that they didn't realize the statue had a recorded message inside. But they feel a sense of relief at the same time.

"Wow, that's really cool!" says Rufus.

"Yeah, cool," mimics Squeaky.

"Yes, it's beyond cool, boys. I hope one day you'll both know how important this message is to everyone on the planet—the two of you included." says Tae Kwon Dog. "Well, I'll see you at practice. I think you're ready now to learn the secret."

"We'll be here!" exclaims Rufus as Squeaky nods affirmatively.

The Master walks them out and smiles his knowing smile as he closes the door behind them.

Later that night, the brothers are once again nestled in their beds, laughing about their mistake.

"How could we be so stupid not to

know the statute was talking?" asks an exasperated Rufus.

"Yeah, stupid," agrees Squeaky as Rufus turns out the light.

"Night, Squeaky."

Squeaky chimes back, "Night, Rufus."

The brothers are almost asleep when a hauntingly familiar voice fills the room:

"What you do to me, you do to thee. We are one."

"Rufus! Rufus! Did you hear that?" cried Squeaky from under his sheets.

"Shut up, Squeaky, just go to sleep!" Rufus snaps back, then mutters under his breath. "Holy Moly!"

CHAPTER SEVEN

The Power Within

Doggedly determined to follow in the paws prints of his Master, Max has been practicing hard at Tae Kwon Do. He's been taking extra classes and when he's at home, Dan will often find him striking a particular stance he's been trying to do perfectly. Although he's putting serious effort into his practice, he's still not as good as the Ratwailer brothers.

Maybe it's their inbred strength

and muscular build, but they also have a gracefulness that has even surprised Tae Kwon Dog. With their natural abilities and an obsession to learn the Master's secret, their progress has been amazing— and frustrating to Max who wants with all his heart to be as good as or better than they are.

The mischievous brothers know how anxious Max gets and love playing tricks on him. They'll tease him to upset him which causes him to make mistakes. And sometimes when Max practices breaking boards, they'll pull the board away at the last minute sending Max flying across the room. The Master sees their bad behavior, but rather than call attention to it or punish them, he wants Max to learn to stand up to the brothers himself.

Tomorrow is Promotion Day and all the students of the dojang will be displaying their knowledge of the sport to reach their next belt level. From beginners through black belts, the students will treat their family and friends to an energetic show of spins, kicks, sparring, and board-breaking. Knowing how much his being there means to Max, Dan is going to close the garage for the day and is looking forward to seeing him in action.

When Dan goes outside to throw out the trash, he expects to see Max practicing his stances. Instead he sees him lying next to the stinky old tires; a pile of empty pizza boxes nearby.

"Max, what's going on? Why aren't you

practicing?" asks a surprised Dan.

Max looks up sadly at Dan, sighs heavily and puts his head back down on his paws.

Dan waves him over. "Come here, Max, I want to show you something."

Max, his belly full of pizza, struggles to get up. He's had his cast off for weeks, but sometimes he feels like it's still there. The two go into the garage and Dan pulls back the dusty curtain to his shop. Behind it sits the Mayor's shiny red vintage car fixed like new.

"Looks pretty good, doesn't she?" exclaims a beaming Dan.

Max gasps and clears his throat. Dan can see his eyes are wet as Max looks away and scratches himself nervously.

"Oh, it's okay boy!" Dan leans down

and gives Max a gentle ear rub. "The Mayor is coming later today to pick it up so he can drive it in the Police and Firefighters' Parade this weekend."

Max raises his head and their eyes meet. Once Dan reprimanded him for his mistake, he never brought it up again. Of course, there were consequences for his actions. Max had to do extra work around the garage, like washing and waxing the cars after Dan fixed them. It was exhausting but fun to work alongside his best friend. He also had to bring Dan the newspaper every morning—something Dan had never asked him to do in the past, but Max was glad to do it.

By not sending him back to the shelter, Max knew he meant more to Dan than the Mayor's car. At first, he didn't believe it, but

now he understood. Dan was his family—
and Max would never leave him.

Max wags his tail low and heads back
over toward the pile of tires.

"Max, where are you going?" Dan
asks shaking his head. "It's not like you to
hang around back like that anymore—and
shouldn't you be practicing?"

Max sighs and looks up at Dan.
Without a word, he goes back over by the
tires and flops down on his side.

Early the next morning, Max presses
his uniform and neatly folds the long white
belt putting it in the pocket. He wonders if
by some stroke of luck he'll get a new belt
today—in the color yellow—meaning that

he's no longer an absolute beginner.

"Max, hurry up, we're going to be late," calls Dan.

Max turns off the iron and climbs the stairs to the kitchen where Dan is reading the newspaper and enjoying his morning coffee. Max wishes he could talk to humans as easily as Tae Kwon Dog does. He clears his throat and stammers.

"D-D-Dan, I was thinking, maybe you shouldn't come today," he says quietly.

Dan looks up from his paper. "Are you serious? It's your first promotion—I don't want to miss it."

Then, putting the paper down, he asks, "What's up Max? Oh, I get it, you're nervous. Well, that's natural. Don't worry, you'll do fine. Hey, everyone will have their friends and family there today. I wouldn't let you down, buddy."

Max smiles weakly up at Dan.

"Oh great," he mutters as he rubs his head against Dan's knee thanking him for his support. He worries that he's going to let Dan down—again. In all his time practicing, Max hasn't broken a board yet. He'll have to do it today to pass his test and be promoted to the next belt level. He's afraid he'll be the only one who doesn't pass, and that he'll embarrass himself and Dan.

At the dojang, people are lined up along the walls to see their favorite students perform. The Ratwailers are practicing together side by side. Although they have no family or friends in attendance, they look confident and excited to show their stuff. Their moves are graceful and their stances are strong.

The Master enlists Max and another student to hold the boards for the brothers as they do their sidekicks. Max is tempted to pull the board away at the last minute like they've done to him so many times in the past, but he looks over at Tae Kwon Dog who is smiling at him in his knowing Master way.

First, Rufus kicks and the crowd applauds as the board cracks and drops to the ground. Next comes Squeaky who also snaps the board in half with a deliberate kick. Again, the crowd claps and hoots their support.

As the Ratwailers bask in their glory, Max is in a kneeling position on the sidelines when he hears Tae Kwon Dog call his name and motion him to come forward.

Max shouts "Yes Sir!" and runs to the center of the floor, standing straight with arms at his side, then bows to the Master.

For his first test, Tae Kwon Dog asks him to recite the Five Tenets of Tae Kwon Do.

This is something the students usually do in unison in class.

Max knows the tenets but can't think of one word. His mind seems empty. Then he hears the Ratwailer brothers chuckling and is tempted to scratch.

The Master hushes them sternly. "Go on Max."

Max takes a long deep breath and from somewhere inside of himself, he begins.

"Courtesy. Integrity. Perseverance." He stops for a minute and barks. Whoops, he didn't mean to do that! He nods at the Master and continues, "Self-Control and... and... Abdominal Spirit."

The students break into laughter at the funny mistake.

"Try again, Max," prompts Tae Kwon Dog.

"Ah, ah, In... In... Indomitable Spirit!" exclaims Max, then quickly looks down at the floor.

The Master nods to Max and asks him to continue to his forms. He completes them almost perfectly. At his final form, his paw slips out from under him throwing him a little off balance. The audience gasps, then cheers for him when he quickly recovers and returns to a strong stance. Max sweats, because he knows the toughest part is yet to come. The Master motions the Ratwailer brothers to the floor to hold the board for Max's kick. Max is worried that they'll pull it away like they often do, but he has no choice but to continue his test. He looks over at Dan who nods his support. He remembers how easy the Ratwailers made it look.

Thinking about them, Max is immediately intimidated and feels off balance as he begins his stance. He stops, breathes, and begins again.

He mounts his stance, swiftly spins, and delivers a strong side kick squarely to the board. The room is silent, and it takes a moment before he realizes nothing has happened. Max stands back with his arms at his side and looks down.

"Every student is allowed two attempts at breaking the board," announces the Master from his spot on the podium. Max looks up at him in disbelief. He has to go through this humiliation again? Tae Kwon Dog nods and motions for him to proceed.

Max quickly wipes the sweat from his eyes with both paws. Briefly he looks in the mirror and for a moment thinks he sees a tiger! Max shakes his head and sees his own reflection.

Once again, he approaches the Ratwailers holding the board between them. Max steadies himself and mounts his stance.

Just before he is about to kick, he hears Rufus say just loud enough for Max to hear, "Think of it as rice paper."

At first, Max doesn't know why he said it or what he means by it. Then it dawns on him.

He regains his composure and concentrates on the board. In his mind he thinks of it as a translucent piece of rice paper. He can see its wafer-thin texture and fragile nature as the light from the windows and skylight reflects through it. Some coughs and murmurs come from the crowd as they wait for Max to make his move.

In the next moment, Max spins and delivers another strong, deliberate side kick, hitting the board just as hard and squarely as the first time. But this time, a loud crack announces that it has split and fallen to the floor.

The crowd explodes in applause. Dan jumps to his feet hooting and hollering.

"Way to go, Max!"

Max bows to the smiling Tae Kwon Dog and can't help letting a small bark slip out.

No one is more surprised than Max that he has split the board, except maybe for the Ratwailer brothers. They both heard Rufus say those words – but neither of them even thought them! "Think of it as rice paper." What does that mean? Neither of them has any idea! It's all so mysterious! But whatever it means, it helped Max earn his belt and for some reason both brothers are very happy about that. So much so, they both gave Max big slaps on the back after he made his promotion.

In the following weeks, other things begin happening that the Ratwailers also can't figure out. For some reason, they stop stealing random food and consciously eat more fruits and vegetables which makes them lose weight. Now their uniforms fit perfectly and they are even more awesome when they perform. Then Squeaky does something totally out of character. He tells Tae Kwon Dog he needs to make some extra money and asks if he can help out at the dojang. At first, the Master is a little uneasy about having him around, knowing his history of bad behavior, but he decides to give him a chance.

For weeks Squeaky washes floors, sweeps the walk, and cleans the bathroom. One day as he is leaving, Tae Kwon Dog approaches him.

"Squeaky, you are doing a great job. I'm very pleased that you offered to help around here. May I ask what you're saving for?"

Squeaky bows his head and reaches into his hoodie, pulling out his music player.

"I stole this a while back and want to pay for it."

The Master nods his approval and pats Squeaky on the back.

"Good show, Squeaky!"

Getting approval from the Master feels good to Squeaky. As a matter of fact, both Ratwailer brothers have learned that feeling good about doing good feels better than lying, stealing, or bullying others. Being the toughest guys on the block isn't important any more.

They realize they have a different power when they do the right thing. They have the power to see the world as positive and not feel embarrassed about how they look on the outside because others can see that they are good on the inside. Just like the Master said, their secret power is within—and it has been there all along but they never knew they had it.

CHAPTER EIGHT

Coming to the Mountain

Max folds the vibrant purple belt and sets it up on Dan's bookshelf next to his others in white, yellow, orange, green, and blue. Now in his third year of Tae Kwon Do, Max is an intermediate student working toward his black belt. Each belt he has achieved is truly an accomplishment worthy of respect.

It has taken a while, but Max no longer feels embarrassed that he is less strong or able than the others. He knows he is every bit as powerful as they are because everyone possesses their own power within.

To celebrate Max's recent achievement, Dan's throwing a party in his honor at his favorite restaurant—Pizza Perfecto. Max is excited because there will be fresh pizza, made to order, not leftovers! All of the students from the dojang are coming, including the Ratwailer brothers. Rufus and Squeaky haven't been near the garage since the Mayor's car incident, and Max has never brought it up again. He knows they are sorry for what they did, and it won't do any good to remind them of their mistake.

Tae Kwon Dog is the Master of

Ceremonies for the event and will be presenting Max with a special gift for his new purple belt status.

Everyone piles into the restaurant and takes a seat around the large family-style tables.

Max sits down next to Dan and an empty chair for the Master. Max wonders what his gift could be? Why he does he need to give him anything at all he wonders. The Master has already given him so much. If it wasn't for him, Max wouldn't be the happy, calm, and contented dog he is today.

When Tae Kwon Dog arrives, everyone stands and cheers. Because of his height, you can barely see him moving between the tables, but with the swiftness of a 9th Dan black belt, he soon appears on the chair next to Max. Rarely seen out of his uniform, Tae Kwon Dog is comfortably dressed in his weekend gear—jeans, sneakers, and with his camera hanging around his neck.

Max swoons as he eats his pizza, delighting in every bite. Afterward he barks his approval.

Dan laughs and gives Max a big hug. His loving gesture surprises Max because Dan rarely shows affection aside from a scratch on the head—and never in public.

Tae Kwon Dog stands on his chair and addresses the room.

"Our friend Max has received his purple belt in Tae Kwon Do which means he's come to the mountain. He is like a tree in mid-growth and now his path becomes steep. Let's join him on his journey by offering our love and support."

The Master reaches inside his camera bag and brings out a sleek gold tiger with ebony stripes. "Let the power of the tiger give you strength on your journey, Max."

Cheers and clapping fill the room. Max gasps when he sees the tiger—his animal spirit—the totem of his dreams. He is overwhelmed with emotion, but sniffs away any trace of tears. He's not going to cry in front of all of these people! Instead, he stands and bows to the Master and accepts his gift graciously.

Long after dinner, everyone has left the restaurant except for Dan and Tae Kwon Dog who are still talking quietly together. In front of them, the tiger sprawls regally on the table casting its mysterious golden glow. Max looks out the window for a moment and catches a glimpse of a scrawny, black-and-white dog going through the trash cans. Without hesitation, he goes outside.

"Are you hungry, friend?" asks a sympathetic Max. "Let's go inside."

Later at home, Max feels great curled in his bed with his golden tiger tucked under his arm. He hopes Dan doesn't notice. He might think it's a silly puppy thing to do.

While drifting off to sleep, Max thinks about his party and the good friends he's made at the dojang. Even Rufus and Squeaky have become buddies. Long ago they had stopped teasing him and they all helped each other learn and grow. Today he was surprised to see them helping clear the plates—without even licking them! Though, it was Tae Kwon Dog who surprised him most of all. Max can't believe that the Master knows him so well that he actually knows what he dreams! In that moment he realizes Tae Kwon Dog has amazing powers that humans don't possess. Max is so grateful Tae Kwon Dog is his Master and mentor.

Deep in his dreams, Max sees himself as a sleek, muscular tiger with magical

powers to heal, comfort, and protect those he loves, and those who are less fortunate. Although to access his inner powers, he must first climb an enormous mountain that reaches thousands of feet up into the clouds. Sitting at the base of the mountain, with his powerful tail tucked beneath him, he breathes deeply and ponders how he will get to its top.

Just then in the stillness of his mind he hears a calm, familiar voice.

"Think of it as rice paper."

THE END

Bokkens

Tae Kwon Dog's Guide to Words, Terms and Characters

access
To retrieve, acquire or gain (gain access to).

adviser or advisor
A person who gives advice in a particular field—"the military adviser to the President" or, in a school, college or university, a teacher who helps a student plan a course of study. "My advisor suggested I switch classes."

agility
The ability to move quickly and easily. Also, to think and understand quickly.

anticipation
The feeling of anticipating or expecting something to happen.

Beethoven concerto
A musical composition by the great

German composer and pianist Ludwig van Beethoven. One of the most admired composers in the history of Western music, his music is among the most performed in classical music.

bask in glory
Enjoying the attention from succeeding at something.

black belt
A black belt in *Tae Kwon Do* means you have mastered the basics of this martial art. You should be very proud of your accomplishment.

bokkens
Japanese wooden swords used in martial arts training. Bok is 'wood' and ken is 'sword'.

breakdance
Breakdancing, also called breaking, is an athletic style of street dance born in the U.S. It mainly consists of four kinds of

movement: toprock, downrock, power moves, and freezes.

Caleb
Energetic, young *Tae Kwon Do* student who is short in height but tall on talent.

careening
To sway dangerously to one side out of control.

Central Park
An urban park in New York City than spans from the Upper East Side to the Upper West Side of Manhattan.

dan
The dan ranking system used by Japanese and Korean martial arts organizations. It refers to a person's level of ability.

Dan
Max's gentle, kind and hard-working human companion who owns the auto repair shop.

distinctive
Some characteristic that makes a person or thing stand out. "His deep voice was distinctive among the others in the band."

dobok
Uniform worn by practitioners of Korean martial arts. Do means way and bok means clothing.

doggedly
Persistently, decisively, stubbornly.

dojang
Formal gathering place for students of Korean martial arts to conduct training and examinations called promotions.

exasperated
To be intensely annoyed and frustrated.

feverishly
In an overly excited or energetic manner.

hip hop
Popular music originally performed by inner-city African Americans and Latino Americans in The Bronx, a borough of New York City in the early 1970s.

hydraulic
Operated by a liquid moving in a confined space under pressure. Relating to the science of hydraulics.

inbred
Naturally existing in a person, animal, or plant from birth.

intimidated
Overly timid or scared by someone or something.

intuitive
Using intuition or a sense of feeling something to be true even without fact. "He had an intuition about where to find his dog that had gone missing."

lumbering
Moving in a slow, heavy, awkward way.

Manhattan
Referred to as The City or the heart of the Big Apple. Manhattan is the most densely populated of New York City's five boroughs which also includes The Bronx, Brooklyn, Queens, and Staten Island.

Max
Gentle, sweet dog who is large in size but feels small in life.

meditation
The act of concentrating on your breathing to quiet your thoughts.

menacing
Gives the feeling of the presence of danger. Threatening, alarming. "His strong, dark eyebrows give his face an oddly menacing look."

mentor
An experienced and trusted adviser.

mimic
To imitate someone in their actions or words. "The class would mimic the teacher's dance moves until they became familiar with them."

native language
Language we learn in early childhood that is spoken in our family or the region where we live. Also known as a mother tongue.

punctuate
To accentuate or emphasize.

Ratwailer Brothers
Rufus and Squeaky are a mischievous pair who look like a cartoon version of the handsome dog breed called Rottweiler.

regards
Thinks of someone or something in a

specified way. "Watching her cook, he regards his mother affectionately."

rice paper
A see-through paper-like material from East Asia made from different plants that is used in painting and baking.

roadster
Fast, sporty car that comes in both left- and right-hand drive.

runt of the litter
A term that refers to the smallest and weakest of a litter of animals.

savor
To taste food or a beverage and enjoy it completely.

seamless
Smooth and continuous, with no apparent gaps or spaces between one part and the next.

solo program
An exercise or program performed alone.

South Korean flag
Features four colors: white, black, red, and blue. The white background is a traditional color in Korean culture that symbolizes purity and peace. The black trigrams each represent a celestial body - heaven, sun, moon, and earth as well as the four virtues of humanity, justice, intelligence, and courtesy. The yin-yang symbol in the middle represents the positive (red) and negative (blue) balance of the universe.

suppress
To keep in or try to make uncomfortable feelings or emotions go away.

tae kwon do
The martial art known for its above shoulder height kicks and spins actually means 'the way of the foot and fist' or 'the way of kicking and punching'. More specifically,

'taekwondo' means the right way of using all parts of the body to stop fights, and help build a better and more peaceful world.

Tae Kwon Dog
Wise, powerful, and patient teacher of Tae Kwon Do. Master of the dojang.

take out in trade
A slang expression that refers to the act of bartering, or doing something for someone in exchange for goods and services.

the pound
A shelter where stray, lost, or abandoned animals, mostly dogs and cats are kept until someone adopts them.

totem
A natural object or animal considered a spirit being or sacred object that serves as a family or tribe emblem or a personal spiritual symbol.

vintage

A term that refers to something from an earlier generation. The word *antique* refers to something that's over 100 years old.

Diane and Otto ©*Diane DiRoberto*

Published writer and photographer Diane DiRoberto (www.dianediroberto.com) enjoyed a long career as a freelance copywriter in New York City, working with prominent advertising agencies and clients including *Sotheby's, Christie's Great Estates, American Express, Ralph Lauren* and *Estée Lauder.* After relocating to New Mexico in 1995, Diane opened *The Darkroom,* a black-and-white rental darkroom serving Santa Fe's robust community of photographers. In Santa Fe she was introduced to Tae Kwon Do, and was impressed by the young students who were excelling at this challenging martial art form. In 2008, Diane returned to the east and now lives in Penfield, New York where she writes from home for international clients and works on personal projects close to her heart.

"One day while I was doodling with my dog Otto by my side, I imagined him as a superhero with a secret power. A sleek black-and-tan Miniature Pinscher, Otto was a sweet and funny character, but fierce to the bone. Ten pounds of solid muscle and determination, he reminded me of a canine version of a *Tae Kwon Do* black belt. I loved dressing him in costumes and thought he'd look great in a martial arts uniform so I drew him in a dobok—and **Tae Kwon Dog** was born!

Now, years later, the wonderful artist Susan Szecsi helps bring **Tae Kwon Dog** to life in *The Power Within*."

- Diane DiRoberto, Author

For more information and upcoming events, please visit:
www.TaeKwonDogBooks.com

Susan in Australia, feeding a wallaby

Susan Szecsi (say-tshee) is an award-winning illustrator and graphic designer. Susan grew up in Hungary, where she completed her studies in classical art at two prestigious Hungarian Art Studios.

During her childhood, her family had several dogs and Susan also had pet parakeets, cats, bunnies, and even a pet chicken—she has always loved animals and appreciated their many different qualities and quirks. Today, she finds companionship in her drawings of whimsical animal characters while never missing the opportunity to make friends with the many non-human inhabitants in her city and countryside.

Susan's clients include *Scholastic, Stanford University, University of California San Francisco, Blue Dot Kids Press, Chicago Review Press, Santa Fe Writers Project*, and many others.

Susan has two sons and currently lives with her husband in the beautiful San Francisco Bay Area of California.

Visit Susan's portfolio on
www.brainmonsters.com,
follow her on Instagram
@susan_szecsi

Made in the USA
Middletown, DE
12 February 2024